The Woman at the Well

How One Encounter Changed a City

WES C. JACKSON

THE WOMAN AT THE WELL
published by Third Ralph Publishing

ISBN: 0615915795
ISBN-13: 978-0615915791

CONTENTS

PREFACE

The story of the woman at the well is rich in revelation. The abundance that Jesus released while there for two days impacted the rest of history.

As you read this story, think about any prejudices and preconceived ideas you might hold. Are any of those ideas holding you back from a true relationship with God? Are they holding you back from a true worship experience?

In ancient times, as in the present, there were cultural norms everyone was expected to adhere to. Would any of those norms have been as important as the revelation Jesus was bringing to the Earth? Do today's norms prevent people from experiencing true spiritual freedom?

A good friend once told me that her idea of parenting was to help transition the child from a state of depending completely on the parent, to depending completely on God. That's a good attitude for a parent to have, and it's a good attitude for teachers and spiritual leaders to have also. If people depend on the person who initially spoke into their lives for their continued spiritual freedom, then they are not free at all. The Bible says that when Jesus sets you free, you are indeed free (John 8:36). It doesn't say that about the rest of us. If I set you free, you aren't really free unless I somehow show you the way to Jesus and help you depend on God for your continued freedom.

Here's the irony – God chooses to work through people to set other people free. So, someone will speak into your life to initially make you free, but you'll only be really free if you see that the gift came not from that person, but through them. The gift of your freedom came from God. It is in that mindset that you will truly be free.

In your freedom, remember to continue having Godly relationships (Hebrews 10:25). Your freedom depends on God, but that shouldn't mean you become isolated. Your freedom is meant to catch on, which can only happen if you stay engaged with the society around you and foment the kind of freedom that radically changed you from a person bound by condemnation to a person who can rejoice in a new and permanent life of joy and bliss.

Let the revelation of Christ spring up within you and become a river of living water, blessing all to whom it flows.

1 ~ IT BEGINS

John 4:1-6   Therefore when the Lord knew that the Pharisees had heard that Jesus was making and baptizing more disciples than John (although Jesus Himself was not baptizing, but His disciples were), He left Judea and went away again into Galilee. And He had to pass through Samaria. So He came to a city of Samaria called Sychar, near the parcel of ground that Jacob gave to his son Joseph; and Jacob's well was there. So Jesus, being wearied from His journey, was sitting thus by the well. It was about the sixth hour.

John 4:7 There came a woman of Samaria to draw water. Jesus said to her, "Give Me a drink."

Jesus engaged the woman in conversation. The Lord started this with her. She was following her routine as she probably did every day, but this day, the Lord met her. She didn't need to do anything out of the ordinary to meet the Lord. He asked her for something she could give, and something that was natural.   He didn't request of her something

3

superhuman in origin. She didn't need anything she didn't already have in order to respond to the Lord's offer of connection.

GOD SPEAKS TO US ALL THE TIME

Have you ever had an idea you thought might change the world, but before you could do anything with it you find out someone you never met had the same idea, and is actually doing the idea? Have you ever had a thought in quiet meditation that to you was a profound revelation, and then someone in your life shared the same thought with you? How did they get the same idea as you? Is it possible they were tuned in to the voice of God just the same way you were? Did you both tune in on purpose, or was it just a moment when your own thoughts were quiet enough to let God's voice break in?

The Lord speaks to people all the time. We don't really get that idea from popular western religious frameworks. In the media we're exposed to, God speaks to one in a billion special people, and the rest of us have to climb the mountain of prayer, meditation and good works if we want a word from God. That's just not the way it really is at all. God wants to speak with you, not just to you. He wants a relationship, and He is out there initiating relationship with people all the time.

That's just what happened at the well. The woman was going about her daily business when the Lord initiated relationship. She didn't have to wait for a prophet like Isaiah or John the Baptist to come to her and tell her about God. Here was the Son of God Himself speaking directly to her.

That type of interaction was not just for a 33-year

period of time at the beginning of a new dispensation. It was for always, and is for always. Even in the Old Testament, there are stories of people who heard from God and allowed Him to initiate a relationship that they then enjoyed all their lives. Read the stories about Samuel (1 Samuel 3), Obed-Edom (2 Samuel 6), and Jeremiah (Jeremiah 1). The Lord called to Samuel. The Lord blessed the house of Obed-Edom when the ark was staying there. The word of the Lord came to Jeremiah. None of these people were going about seeking the encounter that was about to come to them. They were simply doing what was normal to them at the time, when the Lord spoke to them.

2 ~ GOD IS GOOD

John 4:8-9 For His disciples had gone away into the city to buy food. Therefore the Samaritan woman said to Him, "How is it that You, being a Jew, ask me for a drink since I am a Samaritan woman?" (For Jews have no dealings with Samaritans.)

The woman was a little surprised to see this Man not observing the traditions of the time. The division between the Jews and Samaritans ran deep. It was even surprising enough to the disciples that Jesus even wanted to go through that area that they made note of it in the account of the journey (John 4:4).

The breach between the Jews and Samaritans began in 1 Kings 11 when the Lord spoke through Ahijah that He would split the kingdom, because Solomon and the people had forsaken the Lord. This was brought to pass when Rehoboam took the throne in 1 Kings 12. Rehoboam went against the counsel of the elders and created division so deep that the Northern tribes split from Judah. The Northern tribes became the Samaritans, and for a while their capitol was located in Sychar (also called Shechem).

This was where God appeared to Abraham and gave him the promise of the land, and an inheritance, and a great posterity (Genesis 12:7). It was where the sons of Jacob avenged the violation of their sister, Dinah (Genesis 34). It was where the family was living when Joseph was sold to the Egyptians (Genesis 37). Shechem is in the hill country of Ephraim and Manasseh (the place where Caleb wanted to settle), and is where Joseph's tomb is located (Joshua 24:32). This was a place of promise and struggle – a place of worship and a place of war.

Jesus came bringing reconciliation (2 Corinthians 5:18, 19). He reconciled the world to Himself, "not counting their trespasses against them." He wasn't held back by the past, by the problems that had occurred in the area. He brought back together that which had been torn apart. We have, through Christ, the ministry of reconciliation. The works that Jesus did set the example for how we ought to love and serve others also.

Here is a principle to remember always: God is good, all the time. Jesus came to save the world, not to condemn it. Whenever you read a scripture that seems dark or unclear, remember to view it through this lens. If a possible interpretation would mean that God was not good at that time, then that is the wrong interpretation.

God is always good. He is just, and there are many stories of judgment in the Bible, but look more broadly and you will see this consistent truth throughout the Bible: God is always good. He has always been working to reconcile the world to Himself. Jesus here did an act of reconciliation, which would more fully blossom later on through the ministry of the Apostles and the early church.

In Acts 10, Peter had a vision of a sheet being let down with all kinds of four-footed animals. "A voice said to him, 'Get up, Peter. Kill and eat!'" (Acts 10:13). When Peter objected over the law not allowing him to eat certain things, the voice said, "What God has cleansed, no longer consider unholy" (Acts 10:15). After this, Peter realized that God was calling the apostles to reach out not only to the Jews, but also to the Gentiles. In Mark 7:19, Jesus declared all foods clean. Peter would have been there for that, but still had a problem with eating food not approved by the law. Jesus had told the disciples that food isn't what makes a person clean or unclean, but what proceeds out of a man. In the same way, God made it clear that it was not the origin of a person's birth that mattered, but their response to the Holy Spirit and belief in Jesus that is important.

What should be evident here is that God is bringing people out of a mindset of division, and into a mindset of unity. To be reconciled means to be brought back together. To be made whole again. To be reunited. How would Jesus, being a Jew, ask for something from a Samaritan woman? Through the ministry of reconciliation.

3 ~ HOW GREAT A GIFT

How great was the gift Jesus was offering? How great a person did the woman perceive Him to be?

John 4:10 Jesus answered and said to her, "If you knew the gift of God, and who it is who says to you, 'Give Me a drink,' you would have asked Him, and He would have given you living water."

Here's where the revelation really starts flowing. Jesus introduces her to the concept of "living water," which she will have by the end of the story. Imagine if you will that this woman was not entirely resistant to a touch from God, and that everything Jesus says here is true: that if she knew who this was, she would have asked Him for something completely special.

As a side note: Remember the story of Abraham's servant finding Rebecca at the spring (Genesis 24)? Women drawing water in the Bible often are more perceptive and receptive to the Lord than the reader would initially assume.

What would living water even be? Did the woman have any way to understand that type of thing? How would you process something like that if you were hearing it for the very first time? How have you processed new revelations as they came to you? Think about the overwhelming feeling of hearing a new word — something entirely new. Now, put yourself into a social situation — it's another physical person telling you, rather than something you're realizing in meditation. To add to it, make it an awkward social situation that culturally might not be readily accepted if a third person were to arrive. If you consider all this, you realize that the woman handles the situation with a good measure of grace.

John 4:11 She said to Him, "Sir, You have nothing to draw with and the well is deep; where then do You get that living water?

I've heard this passage read with a degree of sass before, as if the woman were mocking. Up to this point, there isn't any reason to suspect otherwise, but trust me for the time being. As the story unfolds, the woman behaves in a way that shows she has more depth than that.

She is asking in earnest. What is living water? Where do you get it? From a natural point of view, Jesus didn't even seem to have the ability to get regular water from the well, so where was He going to get this "living water"?

4 ~ GREATER THAN

John 4:12 "You are not greater than our father Jacob, are You, who gave us the well, and drank of it himself and his sons and his cattle?"

Jacob would have had to have many servants dig the well for many weeks in order to get to the depth it was at when the people were using it. The well is still there today and was originally about 105 feet deep and had 15 feet of water in it. (Tourists have thrown so many pebbles into it that today it is only about 65 feet deep and has no standing water.) The well is 7.5 feet in diameter. Given those dimensions, the material removed from the ground to make the well would have totaled about 4636 cubic feet, or about 171 cubic yards. A 10-wheel dump truck can hold about 10-12 cubic yards of dirt, so this would have been about 14-17 trips for today's dump trucks to get all the material from the dig site. All this would have weighed around 280 to 340 tons.

Imagine the effort to do the same thing with

shovels, picks, wheelbarrows and wagons in Jacob's day! So, when the woman at the well asked Jesus if He was greater than Jacob, this was the yardstick of greatness she had in mind. To translate into today's terms, "Are you sufficiently influential or wealthy that you could have hundreds of people working for weeks to remove this material, shore up the shaft, install a dome cover, and ring the well with a bench? Are you the type of person who could initiate, direct and complete the undertaking of one of the most important public works in the area?"

The greatness of Jesus Christ surpasses all worldly greatness. When He ran the money changers out of the temple, the people challenged His authority to do that. His response was, "Destroy this temple, and in three days I will raise it up" (John 2:19). He was referring to His resurrection, which would have been impossible for Solomon or Ezra or Zerubbabel to perform in their own power, even though they had the civic power to have built the temple – Solomon having built the first temple, and Ezra and Zerubbabel having supervised the reconstruction after the return from captivity (Ezra 6:15). Is Jesus greater than Solomon, or Ezra or Zerubbabel? Yes!

5 ~ WILL YOU THIRST AGAIN?

If I gave you a cup of religion to drink, you would be thirsty again and come back to me for more. But, if I gave you a cup of life, not only would you not thirst again, but you would spread life to others who will no longer thirst either.

John 4:13 Jesus answered and said to her, "Everyone who drinks of this water will thirst again; . . ."

The answer here immediately casts all that Jacob did in proper context with what Jesus was offering. The favor God had shown Jacob was truly great. He had become prosperous enough to direct a public work that would have freed him from dependence on his neighbors for water. Yet as great as this was, it was also true that this water was only sufficient for quenching immediate thirst. A person who drank from Jacob's well, as special as it was, would still be thirsty again. Jesus' answer to the question of whether He was greater came in the form of a contrast between the greatness of the water from the well, and the surpassing greatness of the living water.

John 4:14 ". . . but whoever drinks of the water that I will give him shall never thirst; but the water that I will give him will become in him a well of water springing up to eternal life."

The truth in this passage is so rich that the rest of the chapter hinges on its importance. What Jesus is offering here is the kind of gift that keeps on replicating itself. You can come to a physical well and get your thirst quenched for the day, but you'll have to come back again soon. You can come to an elaborate religious experience that impresses you and makes you feel like you got filled up, but you'll have to keep coming back to that source once you go dry again. What Jesus offers is something more – something man cannot create on his own without the Spirit.

How have your spiritual experiences been? Were you hungry for more in a way that made you want to continue growing in relationship and as a person, or were you hungry to repeat the same experience you just had?

If you go to a great music concert, you may for days want to go back and re-live some of the highlights. You'll probably tell all your friends about it, share pictures and videos, and listen to the band's songs more than usual. That's all great, but does it make you want to become a better musician, or just go to more concerts?

Church can be the same way. We can have an amazing time in a service, but what does it do long-term? Are we hungry for more of God, and have a desire to go deeper, or are we "hungry" for a repeat of the same thing we just had? Do we want more true relationship, or just an emotional and experiential fix that we can produce by the sights and sounds of a well-orchestrated service?

I say this with all due respect for the modern church. I'm part of it. We reach a lot of people and they come and experience something that at least at first seems like freedom. But it's only real if they stay free, and if their freedom doesn't depend on hearing something pleasing, or having a rock concert experience. If their dreams change, if their life changes, and if they are truly filled like the sail of a great ship with the wind of the Holy Spirit, then they have had a true encounter.

6 ~ DIG THE WELL

Now comes the time to dig the well that will spring up to eternal life.

John 4:15 The woman said to Him, "Sir, give me this water, so I will not be thirsty nor come all the way here to draw."

The woman did not delay in asking for the gift. She has been inquisitive so far, and has not turned away Jesus' offer of connection. Here, she begins to ask for the right thing.

Being open to a gift from God is an admirable trait. The woman had no reason to ask Jesus for anything except for the inner feeling of connection that must have been starting to build in her. The Bible doesn't say what she was thinking right at this moment. Was she saying this to get Jesus to go away, or was she opening herself up to a new experience? What we do know is that she didn't say, "Go away! There's no such thing as living water. You're strange!" She basically said, "Cool! I'd like to try some of that!" This made all the difference.

John 4:16 He said to her, "Go, call your husband and come here."

A classical interpretation of this verse is that, being a woman, Jesus would not continue to deal with her and wanted to, "keep things in order," by dealing with her husband. When did Jesus ever stay beholden to tradition? He healed on the Sabbath! (John 9). He let his disciples eat with unwashed hands! (Matthew 15). He allowed a woman who had led a sinful life to wash His feet with perfume and dry them with her hair! (Luke 7:37). Why, in this instance, would He be trying to stick to the expectations of worldly custom? No, He was not adhering to tradition here. He was giving the woman what she asked for.

Jesus didn't necessarily need to build up to things. Several times in the Bible, people asked Jesus a question, and the very next thing He said was the start of their answer. "Lord, how can we feed this many?" "How many loaves do you have?" (Mark 6:38).

John 4:17, 18 The woman answered and said, "I have no husband." Jesus said to her, "You have correctly said, 'I have no husband'; for you have had five husbands, and the one whom you now have is not your husband; this you have said truly."

The moment she asked for the gift, Jesus began to give it to her. *"The water that I will give him will become in him a well of water springing up to eternal life."* The water in Jacob's well was already there before Jacob or his company ever set foot on the land. Jacob's accomplishment was removing the material that stood between the water and the thirsty people, and ensuring the sides would not collapse, so that generations would be able to come and drink there.

When the woman asked for the water, Jesus began to remove the substance that stood in the way of the living water flowing through her. Isaiah 59:2 says that sin separates people from God. Not only did Jesus start to dislodge the woman's lifestyle from the path in front of her, He did so in a way that stirred faith in her. Romans 14:23 says that what is not of faith is sin. So, even if the woman had been caught in adultery by someone, that type of acknowledgement of sin would only have produced condemnation. The way Jesus did it, she went instantly from a state of separation to a state of connection! Condemnation does not connect us to God. It only connects back to sin. This causes people to live in a destructive loop.

Many people's religious framework leads to a cycle of condemnation, repentance, and condemnation again. How many people immediately start behaving differently in the presence of a church or a person in the ministry? Most of the time, that reaction has more to do with the person's perception of what religion is than it does with the person or place. People have heard that God hates sin, and that they are full of sin, and so He must be unhappy with them. Whenever they think God is looking, they toss their sin on the ground behind them.

The popular, if unspoken, definition of religion is, "Being better than me," when we think we're being bad, and "Being as good as me," when we think we're being good. Both are silly and wrong. God is love (1 John 4:8). The media and many forms of religion teach that God is something else. Those are wrong. God is love. If we come to God thinking He is anything else, we are bound to misunderstand Him. When we learn that God is love, then through a consistent encounter with God, we live in love toward others. This is completely incompatible with the condemnation cycle.

The woman chose the path of receiving love, rather than condemnation, and kept on the path of freedom Jesus was leading her on.

John 4:19 The woman said to Him, "Sir, I perceive that You are a prophet."

She's getting it and is verbally acknowledging that Jesus is not just some thirsty traveler with strange ideas about water. She went from asking for living water, to having rubble made level, to a place of faith and spiritual awareness.

7 ~ WHERE HEAVEN MEETS EARTH

John 4:20 "Our fathers worshiped in this mountain, and you people say that in Jerusalem is the place where men ought to worship."

Notice how the woman never dwelt on the "many husbands" thing. That was in the past now and had been made level (Isaiah 40:4 and John 1:23). Jesus spoke to it and she received it instantly. Now she has moved on to the most important question she could have known to ask at that point.

The division between kingdoms led to intense religious strife. Not only did the Northern kingdom split from the Jews, they set up altars on the high places and worshipped other gods. Jeroboam was eventually destroyed over this, and the Northern kingdom was the first to go into captivity (1 Chronicles 5:25-26). There was disagreement even over where to worship God, with the Jews worshipping in Jerusalem where the temple was, and the Samaritans worshipping on Mount Gerzim. This was a terrible conflict that needed a resolution.

The woman was realizing this was a man of whom she could ask questions of this nature. She wanted to know the truth about really worshipping God, more than any other question she might have had. Plenty of people might have asked something different of a prophet such as might give them advantage in their worldly dealings, but this woman drove right to the heart of what is most important to every human being! Where shall we worship God?

John 4:21 Jesus said to her, "Woman, believe Me, an hour is coming when neither in this mountain nor in Jerusalem will you worship the Father.

It's about to get really interesting. Even though, according the Old Testament and Mosaic law, Jesus could have said that one must go up to Jerusalem for the feasts and other religious observations, He was about to fulfill the law and open the doors to a whole new way to relate to our Creator. The answer says that none of the old conflicts will matter anymore. The old things, both right and wrong, were passing away and a new thing was being brought to pass.

John 4:22 "You worship what you do not know; we worship what we know, for salvation is from the Jews.

If she was wondering which side had been right in the past, it was the Jews. The Lord never said to go off and build an alternative religion. Today's alternative religions are the ones that teach something other than what Jesus is about to say next.

John 4:23 "But an hour is coming, and now is, when the true worshipers will worship the Father in spirit and truth; for such people the Father seeks to be His worshipers.

Now the past no longer matters. What matters is that now the hour had come when the religious systems would no longer suffice. The Father seeks true worshippers. We are not just walking the earth looking for meaning. The Father is seeking those who will worship Him in spirit and truth.

To really appreciate this, we need to look at where the world had come from to get to this point. The arc of history in the Old Testament tells a wonderful story of grace. The Father brought out a deeply religious people from a nation that had enslaved them and subjected them to the oldest form of government: fear. Fear has been the most efficient way to rule over people for as long as there have been human records. There are even cave drawings depicting ancient shamen, deep in the dark recesses of the clan dwelling, performing frightening rituals. A person back then would have been terrified to cross the priest or risk becoming the next human sacrifice. The same has been true in most theocratic civilizations, and has often been true in secular societies throughout history. Julius Caesar found that he could control the mob through carefully balancing fear and benevolence, and subsequent emperors used the gladiatorial games both to entertain and to control the masses.

In Egypt, the Pharaoh was considered by the people to be a god. The Egyptians were highly superstitious and were preoccupied with death and the afterlife. Religious trappings, coupled with cruel taskmasters, made life very hard for slaves.

When the Lord led the people out of Egypt by the hand of Moses, He was taking them from a scary but familiar world, into what would ultimately be a place of complete freedom and prosperity. However, most of the people would not make the transition. The people had lived among Egyptians who worshipped idols made with their hands. The Lord tried to speak to the children of Israel in the wilderness, but they were frightened and asked Moses to speak to God and relay messages to the people (Exodus 20:18-20). So, in Exodus 25, God told Moses to construct an ark, and there His presence would dwell.

God wanted worshippers who would worship Him in spirit and truth, even back then. Remember that God does not change, so this was not something new at the well that had never been thought of before. God had waited until now to be able to take the people to the next step through the long transition to freedom.

The people went from worshipping other gods they had made with their hands (or living among people who did so), to worshipping the true God who, in His mercy, appeared above the mercy seat on an ark He had them make. Now Jesus was opening the door for the woman to see that the time had come for the true worshippers to worship, not at a place where there is an ark and where God had only limited interaction with a defined set of people, but in spirit and truth, wherever they might be.

What does it mean to worship in spirit and truth? Not at a place, but in spirit? 1 Corinthians 6:19 says that now we are the temple of the Holy Spirit. Rather than make a pilgrimage to Jerusalem for feasts and to worship according to a ritual, we now get to relate to the Lord intimately, in our own heart, at any time. Worship in the Old Testament was done according to a set pattern. It didn't always have to be that way. David worshipped God in the fields where he tended sheep. Many people throughout the Old Testament worshipped and praised the Lord wherever they were. However, when the congregation came together, the priests and Levites led the gatherings according to a very strict set of prescribed rules that had to be adhered to. One could follow all those rules and worship in body only – not in spirit.

You didn't necessarily have to be "into it," as long as you showed up and went through the motions. That's not the kind of worship the Father desires. That's not relationship. God wants worshippers who really worship Him. That's worshipping in truth. Not going through the motions, but truly worshipping Him with all our being.

Here's possibly the most amazing part: Where does Heaven touch Earth? Wherever you are when you are worshipping – that's where!

What sound does it make? -- What sound do you make?

What does it feel like? -- What do you feel like?

John 4:24 "God is spirit, and those who worship Him must worship in spirit and truth."

This "must" happen. This was no longer an option. The hour had come not to give an alternate path or clear up old disputes, but to declare a new thing on the Earth. "Neither in this mountain, nor in

Jerusalem."

No more alternative religions. No more new sets of rituals to perform. This is the way now and isn't negotiable.

8 ~ START THE WATER FLOWING

John 4:25   The woman said to Him, "I know that Messiah is coming (He who is called Christ); when that One comes, He will declare all things to us."

The woman by this time surely knew that Jesus was someone special. She had perceived He was a prophet and proceeded to ask Him the most important question. Could it be that this was her polite way of asking Him straight out if He was the Christ? Remember that even John the Baptist sent disciples to just go ask and make sure (Matthew 11:3). So, would it not be normal for this woman, in whom Jesus had planted the fast-growing seeds of revelation, to want to hear it plainly?

Sometimes you know inside that something is true, but it helps to hear it anyway. Thomas spent years with Jesus and still needed to see the nail holes himself before he would believe Jesus had truly risen. Not everyone has an easy time going with what they know to be the truth before they hear it. If that's you, it's okay. Jesus didn't reject Thomas. But, He did say that it is even better to believe, even though you haven't seen (John 20:29). Start where you are. If you need to ask, as the woman did, then ask.

John 4:26 Jesus said to her, "I who speak to you am He."

While she must have been anticipating this answer, this had to have overwhelmed the woman with awe. Here she was, talking at the well to Jesus Christ, the Saviour, the Messiah, the Anointed One. Everything that had been written in the sacred texts had anticipated this moment. He didn't even have His entourage or security staff with Him. He was out there alone just finding someone who would be the key to opening up a city, and she had just come to draw water.

9 ~ TIME OUT FOR TRAINING, PART 1

John 4:27 At this point His disciples came, and they were amazed that He had been speaking with a woman, yet no one said, "What do You seek?" or, "Why do You speak with her?"

The disciples had been raised in the same traditions they were now seeing Jesus take down, and it occurred to them that this was somehow odd. However, they had the grace not to say anything or interrupt Jesus while He was ministering. Notice that they didn't jump in right before the woman could ask if Jesus was the Christ and start talking about ministry logistics. Love has timing, and these men had begun to learn when to ask questions and when to wonder quietly.

In your ministry activity, take care to note when the right time is to ask questions, and when you should learn and be in "receive" mode. Don't jump in at the wrong time and interrupt the flow of the Holy Spirit during a sensitive ministry time. Love has timing!

We'll see more about this in Chapter 11.

10 ~ CARRYING THE MESSAGE

John 4:28 So the woman left her water pot, and went into the city and said to the men,

(Not just to the women, but to the men.)

John 4:29 "Come, see a man who told me all the things that I have done; this is not the Christ, is it?"

Jesus told the woman one thing about having had several husbands, but that one word brought down all the walls that separated her from the Lord. Those walls now gone, there was also nothing to separate the people around her from the flow of living water that Jesus had unstopped in the woman.

Notice how polite she still is. Just like she asked if Jesus was the Christ in a very meek and indirect way, here she is telling all the men of the city that she had met the Christ, but she is telling them in a way that they could receive. Even though Jesus was not beholden to all the cultural norms, the people would have responded differently to the woman if she had come in as a judge.

In our walk with God, the Word comes to us and life begins to flow. The woman at the well sets a good example of how to take the next step. Jesus spoke to her, and she went to the city carrying a genuine gratitude and sense of wonder. She didn't speak to the people as if she had been lifted up above them. If anything, she appeared to them as a servant. This is the true model of gospel ministry that Jesus defined. "If anyone wants to be first, he shall be last of all and servant of all" (Mark 9:35).

What would coming in as a judge have looked like? When Lot and his family lived in Sodom, he had little success in turning the people there to the ways of the Lord. When they were getting ready to depart, the men of the city criticized Lot and said that he had come there as a judge. Jesus said later that if the miracles that were done in the cities He ministered in had been done in Sodom, it would still be standing (Matthew 11:23). The woman here approaches her city with the humble heart of a servant, and the result was salvation. In modern times, the city is home to over 120,000 people, and is an important center for trade, culture and the arts. This was a far better outcome than that of Sodom, wouldn't you say?

11 ~ TIME OUT FOR TRAINING, PART 2

John 4:30,31 They went out of the city, and were coming to Him. Meanwhile the disciples were urging Him, saying, "Rabbi, eat."

Now that they were alone with Jesus, the disciples asked about day-to-day stuff. They must have noticed Jesus hadn't eaten anything, and so they urged Him to take some food. Perhaps they realized that the city was coming out to meet Jesus, and thought He might benefit from some nourishment. While one might observe that they did not perceive what Jesus was about to say to them, they at the time did not have the benefit of the next verse as you and I do. They were learning. What is wonderful, though, is that they held their question for an appropriate time.

John 4:32-34 But He said to them, "I have food to eat that you do not know about." So the disciples were saying to one another, "No one brought Him anything to eat, did he?" Jesus said to them, "My food is to do the will of Him who sent Me and to accomplish His work."

Jesus taught the disciples plainly, but still some things were so different from the experience they were used to, that they were initially a mystery. Jesus drew his life's energy from doing the will of the Father. He didn't need physical food right then. He had just been engaged in an amazing ministry time, and it was about to go even deeper.

John 4:35-38   "Do you not say, 'There are yet four months, and then comes the harvest'? Behold, I say to you, lift up your eyes and look on the fields, that they are white for harvest.   "Already he who reaps is receiving wages and is gathering fruit for life eternal; so that he who sows and he who reaps may rejoice together.   For in this case the saying is true, 'One sows and another reaps.'   I sent you to reap that for which you have not labored; others have labored and you have entered into their labor."

The job that the disciples had to do was not the sum total of all the liberation that God had in mind for the Israelites from the time of Exodus on.   Many had done work to get things to this point, and now they were getting to enter into all that labor.   For thousands of years, people had worked one life at a time to get the people free.   Through wars and captivity, through cycles of religious bondage and disobedience, back to obedience, and back again, the Israelites had gone through a great deal.   Their entire history was etched with a consistent call from God, beckoning them to come to Him.   Now the time was at hand to fulfill what had been promised – to reap the harvest.   The disciples were getting to reap what had been sown and labored for all those centuries.

12 ~ LIVING WATER REVIVES THE CITY

John 4:39 From that city many of the Samaritans believed in Him because of the word of the woman who testified, "He told me all the things that I have done."

The woman from the well had been very effective. This was without any ministry training or college education. She simply went to town and told the people that she had met the One for whom they had all been waiting all their life. The woman had begun to impart to the city the thing that Jesus had imparted to her at the well.

She didn't make it complicated, but just spoke the simple truth. So much of our training effort in modern times is dedicated to removing from our thinking the types of systems that would make it impossible simply to tell a town about Jesus. The gospel is simple. It takes a lot of professional work to make it as complex as most people believe it is. For two millennia, people have tried to add to the gospel, only to have those additions bring bondage where there should be freedom.

John 4:40,41 So when the Samaritans came to Jesus, they were asking Him to stay with them; and He stayed there two days. Many more believed because of His word;

They invited Him in, and He expanded what the woman had started. From many believing, to many more.

John 4:42 and they were saying to the woman, "It is no longer because of what you said that we believe, for we have heard for ourselves and know that this One is indeed the Savior of the world."

This is what makes the whole thing sing. The people in verse 39 believed because of what the woman had said. However, if the water had not been living water, but a religious creation, they would have needed to keep coming back to her for more. Now they had heard for themselves and believed in Jesus through the relationship they had now formed with Him.

It's a simple test. If I give you something and it changes your life and you never have to see me or talk to me again to keep it going, and you can share it with others and the same thing happens, then it was from God. On the other hand, if what I give you makes sense and gets you doing some right things, but you need to keep coming back to me to get more or it quits working, then it was either not living water, or you received it through a lens of condemnation and you connected back to a fallen state rather than to the

Lord.

Remember that it doesn't say that all of them believed. Just that many believed her, and many more believed when they had met Jesus. There were probably a number of people who never believed, even though they heard the same word. The recipients are not a test of the gift. If nobody receives and no life is formed, then it is likely a dead word (or delivered through a dead system), and the result is like Sodom. If some do, even though some don't, then rejoice over the seeds that fell on good soil and produced a crop.

CONCLUSION

Where does the living water come from? It originates from God, and it flows through you. If it is not flowing through you, then allow Jesus to unblock the well in you and let the river flow. Allow the Lord to remove old systems and destructive cycles from your life. Let go of the weight that holds you down, and allow yourself to experience true freedom.

Coming to Jesus is a simple thing. Just come as you are. The woman at the well had no special tools or training for what was about to happen. She was willing to receive what Jesus had to say. A day before, a hard-working journalist might have written that this was a person whom God would never use. She was living with a man she was not married to, and had been married five times before this. None of this mattered to the Lord. What mattered was that in the moment He spoke to her, she listened and received. She became a pure vessel as soon as He unstopped the well.

It is often said that it is human nature to be introspective, and so a person might think it normal to dwell on the past and try to make a plan for how to live right from then on. The woman did not fall into this trap. She instantly grabbed hold of the revelation that was being offered to her, and wanted to know where Heaven meets Earth. "Where do we go to worship?" The good news: in spirit and truth! No more trying to get to the right geographical location to worship the Lord. We can now worship God in the temple of the Holy Spirit, who dwells inside us wherever we are.

Allow yourself the freedom to be free, and let the Lord work through you to spread enduring life wherever you go. May the river of living water flow from your belly!

LIVING WATER IN YOUR LIFE

How does the story of the woman at the well apply in your life? Are there areas of your life that have held back the flow of living water?

Have you been caught in a cycle of condemnation and repentance, leading back to condemnation? Don't let that continue.

You can't cleanse yourself by doing enough righteous acts (Gal 2:21).

The Bible says that Jesus cleanses the church by the "washing of water with the word" (Eph. 5:26). If you have been immersed in things that distract you from your true calling in God, you won't simply remove those things. You can't sustain a vacuum for long (Mat. 12: 43-45). You need to displace the distractions in your life with a steady flow of God's word, and fellowship with people who are doing the same.

Reading this book is a good start. Let Christ open up the well in your life right now. You don't need to do anything special – just let Him in.

The notes pages that follow are there to help you on your journey. Use them to remind yourself how good God is, and how He wants an encounter with you. Use the questions that follow to help start a discussion, or simply reflect on them in your quiet time.

May you live a blessed life, and may you be a blessing to others on your journey.

NOTES:

On the pages that follow, space is made for notes. At the top of each page is a heading to help guide your notetaking.

Read this little book again, and highlight the verses and go look them up yourself. If you borrowed this book or don't want to write in it, see the bibliography page for a list of the verses.

In addition to re-reading this, I encourage you to read the books of John, Galatians and Hebrews. You should read all the Bible, but these three are a wonderful place to start.

In John, you will see an intimate portrait of Jesus' life, written by the "Disciple whom Jesus loved." Jesus and John were like best friends. John wrote from the point of view of a close friend, the way you might write if you were writing about the life of your best buddy, who happened to be the Savior of the World. The other gospel writers wrote from a slightly different point of view. Matthew focused on how the life of Jesus fulfilled the Old Testament prophesies about the Christ. Mark's gospel is shorter than the others, but may have been the first to be written. It tells the story in the form of a historical account. Luke's gospel is a letter to his friend, and has the feel of a personal account. John wrote about his friend and Savior.

The book of Galatians is a letter written to the church in Galatia. The church had fallen into the trap of trying to correct the bad things in their life by doing good deeds according to the Old Testament law, rather than trusting in Jesus. Paul wasn't correcting them for doing good, but rather for trying to be good enough to deserve to continue in their salvation. Many Christians today fall into the same trap.

Hebrews in a wonderful letter that gives an account of the spiritual history of Christ, from the time of Abraham all the way to the fulfillment of the promise in Jesus.

As you read these, come back to the notes pages and make entries based on the heading. For instance, on the page headed, "God is Good," write down things that reinforce your belief that God is Good all the time. On the page titled, "Come as you Are," remind yourself that you don't need to get perfect before you come to God.

If you come across something that you don't understand, ask God to give you the meaning of it. If something seems not to agree with the statements on the notes pages, ask why. Is there more to the story, or is there a context the scripture fits into that you need to learn about? Don't accept that God was ever not good, even for a moment! He is always good, and He always loves you.

GOD IS GOOD

_____

_____

_____

_____

_____

_____

_____

_____

_____

_____

_____

_____

_____

_____

_____

_____

GOD LOVES ME

_____

_____

_____

_____

_____

_____

_____

_____

_____

_____

_____

_____

_____

_____

_____

_____

GOD CAN WORK THROUGH MY LIFE

_____

_____

_____

_____

_____

_____

_____

_____

_____

_____

_____

_____

_____

_____

_____

_____

GOD IS LOVE

_____

_____

_____

_____

_____

_____

_____

_____

_____

_____

_____

_____

_____

_____

_____

_____

COME AS YOU ARE

_____

_____

_____

_____

_____

_____

_____

_____

_____

_____

_____

_____

_____

_____

_____

_____

QUESTIONS FOR GROUP DISCUSSION

1. Do today's norms prevent people from experiencing true spiritual freedom?
2. Am I trying to be superhuman to please God or get His attention?
3. How have I processed new revelations as they came to me?
4. Have I had a revelation about something that another person had at the same time?
5. Am I overly formal about my prayer life?
6. Have I struggled to believe that God is always good?
7. Have I seen people not being good and blamed God?
8. Do I have any prejudices that limit what I will do for God?
9. Are there areas of my life where I need to let God unstop the well?
10. What is living water?
11. What keeps me coming back for more?
12. What new experiences have I allowed myself to have lately?
13. What are my dreams?
14. Are there states of separation in my life that should be turned to connection?
15. Have I ever lived in the destructive loop of condemnation?
16. Do I dwell on things that God has forgiven?
17. What is my worship experience like?
18. Thinking about the kind of spiritual life I have, would I recommend this life to others?

BIBLIOGRAPHY

Scripture references, in order of appearance in the book:
John 4
John 8:36
Hebrews 10:25
1 Samuel 3
2 Samuel 6
Jeremiah 1
1 Kings 11
1 Kings 12
Genesis 12:7
Genesis 34
Genesis 37
Joshua 24:32
2 Corinthians 5:18, 19
Acts 10:13
Acts 10:15
Mark 7:19
Genesis 24
John 2:19
Ezra 6:15
John 9
Matthew 15
Luke 7:37
Mark 6:38
Isaiah 59:2
Romans 14:23
1 John 4:8
Isaiah 40:4
John 1:23
1 Chronicles 5:25-26
John 20:29
Gal 2:21
Eph. 5:26
Matthew 12: 43-45